Good News for Everyone

Retold by Penny Frank

Illustrations by John Haysom

D0262741

LION
Children's Books

The Bible tells us how God sent his Son Jesus to show us what God is like and how we can belong to God's kingdom.

This is the story of what happened to the disciples after Jesus had left them and gone back to be with God.

You can find this story in your own Bible, in the book of Acts, chapters 1 to 4.

Copyright © 1985 Lion Publishing
Illustrations copyright © 1985
John Haysom

Published by
Lion Publishing plc
Sandy Lane West, Oxford, England
www.lion-publishing.co.uk
ISBN 0 7459 4124 9

First edition 1985
Paperback edition 1989
This revised edition 1999
10 9 8 7 6 5 4 3 2 1 0

Printed and bound in Slovenia

Jesus had gone back to heaven to be with God. But his disciples had important work to do. They were to tell the whole world about Jesus!

'You will need God's special help,' Jesus said. 'So go back to Jerusalem and wait there.'

One day, when the disciples were all
together, praying, there was a sudden
noise, as if a gale of wind was rushing
through the house.

Then they saw what looked like
tongues of fire that reached out and
touched each one of them. They looked
at each other in amazement.

They began to speak, and found
themselves talking in languages they did
not even know. They felt very excited
and full of joy.

'God has sent the special help that
Jesus promised us,' they shouted. They
made so much noise that a big crowd
gathered.

The disciples forgot how frightened they had been. Now they wanted to tell the whole world about Jesus and God's kingdom.

Jerusalem was full of visitors from other countries, because it was the festival of Pentecost.

The disciples rushed outside and started to tell the crowd the wonderful story of Jesus.

Everyone could understand. Each of the visitors heard them speaking in his own language!

It was a miracle. God had given the
disciples the special help they needed to
tell the people about the kingdom of
God. They could not see Jesus any more,
but God had sent his Holy Spirit to live
in each of them, always.

7

The most amazing person to watch was
Simon Peter. When Jesus had died,
Simon Peter had been very frightened.
All he had wanted was to go back to
being a fisherman on Lake Galilee.

But now Simon Peter was filled with God's power. He stood up in front of everyone and explained the good news of God's kingdom. His face was shining with joy and gladness.

A few days later, Simon Peter and
another disciple, John, went to the
temple to worship God. They were full of
praise.

They wanted to thank God for the
special help he had given them.

As they went through the gate, they saw
a man who had never been able to walk,
sitting there asking for money.

Every day his friends brought him to
the gate, so that he could beg from the
people who were going to the temple.

11

'Please give me some money,' he called out to Simon Peter and John.

'We don't have any money,' said Simon Peter. 'But we do have something to give you. In the name of Jesus, I tell you to stand up and walk!'

Simon Peter took him by the hand, and the man stood up. His feet and legs became strong. He started to leap and jump about.

He went with them into the temple, shouting praises to God at the top of his voice.

When the people in the temple saw him, they stopped what they were doing.

'Just a minute,' they said, 'aren't you the man who sat at the temple gate? What's happened to you?'

The man told them.

Simon Peter said, 'I don't know why you
are so surprised. We didn't do this by
ourselves. Jesus from Nazareth, whom
you killed, was God's own Son. God
raised him to life again. Now he has
gone back to be with God, but God has
given us his special power.

'Tell God you are sorry for what you
did and he will forgive you. Believe us,
Jesus is alive.'

Many people were excited to hear that
Jesus was still alive, especially the
people who had been healed by him, or
had enjoyed listening to his teaching.

In the city of Jerusalem many people believed the good news of God's kingdom, and God gave them the special power he had given to Jesus.

Day after day, more and more people found that what the disciples were so joyful about was really true. Jesus was still alive!

The priests and leaders in Jerusalem
were horrified to find that the disciples
of Jesus were telling everyone that he
was alive again.

'Stop telling the people about Jesus,' they told Simon Peter and John.

'We can't,' the disciples said. 'Jesus told us to tell the whole world.'

They told everyone they met about Jesus.

More and more people became followers of Jesus. They often met together in the temple, to thank God for his kingdom and his help.

They often had meals together in each others' homes. If anyone was poor, or had no food, the others shared their food or money with them.

They really loved each other. And they
knew it was because God was giving
them his special help.

He had made them into new people,
by giving them his own Holy Spirit.
They were completely changed.

The priests and leaders in Jerusalem made up their minds to stop people talking about God's kingdom. The followers of Jesus were punished. They had to leave the city and go to other towns and villages.

But this was the best thing that could have happened.

It meant that the good news about God's kingdom was now being told to the whole world.

Some Notes for Parents and Teachers

Each book in the *Lion Story Bible* series retells a favourite story from the Old or New Testament.

The New Testament stories tell of the life and teaching of God's Son, Jesus. The stories are about people he met, what he did and what he said. Almost all we know about the life of Jesus is recorded in the four Gospels—Matthew, Mark, Luke and John. The word gospel means 'good news' and this is what Jesus told the first Christians to share with others—a story which continues today all over the world.

Good News for Everyone is from the first chapters of the New Testament book of Acts: the Pentecost story, from chapter 2; the healing of the crippled man, from chapter 3; troubles with the Jewish leaders, from chapter 4.

No one can see God's Holy Spirit. But Jesus had promised that when he went away he would send his Spirit to be with each of his followers for ever. He would show them the truth and help them to live as God wanted.

On the day of Pentecost, Jesus' disciples had no doubt that the Holy Spirit had come. First they heard a sound like a great rushing wind, and saw flames of fire that did not set light to anything. Then they found that, instead of being frightened and hiding away, they were able to stand up in front of great crowds and tell them about Jesus—in their own languages. Nothing, no one, could stop them now!

Other books in the *Lion Story Bible* series retell more of God's story—a story for all time and all people.